RECIPES
from the
VINEYARDS
of
NORTHERN
CALIFORNIA

Asian PASTA

Leslie Mansfield

CELESTIALARTS
Berkeley, California

When preparing recipes that call for egg yolks or whites, whether or not they are to be cooked, use only the highest-quality, salmonella-free eggs.

CELESTIALARTS
P.O. Box 7123
Berkeley, California 94707

Distributed in Canada by Ten Speed Canada, in the United Kingdom and Europe by Airlift Books, in New Zealand by Southern Publishers Group, in Australia by Simon & Schuster Australia, in South Africa by Real Books, and in Singapore, Malaysia, Hong Kong, and Thailand by Berkeley Books.

Cover and interior design by Greene Design
Cover photograph by Larry Kunkel
Photo styling by Veronica Randall
Public Domain Art thanks to Dover Publications

Library of Congress Card Catalog Number 99-80108

First printing, 2000
Printed in the United States

1 2 3 4 5 6 7 —03 02 01 00

To

DORIS MANSFIELD,

*who introduced me to the pleasures
of the garden.*

ACKNOWLEDGMENTS

Deepest gratitude goes to my husband Richard, who has helped me with every step—his name belongs on the title page along with mine. To my wonderful parents, Stewart and Marcia Whipple for their unflagging confidence. To Phil Wood, who makes dreams a reality. To my dear friend and editor Veronica Randall, whose creativity, intelligence, and wit makes working with Celestial Arts a joy. To Victoria Randall, for her invaluable assistance. To Brad Greene, for another spectacular design. To Larry Kunkel, for his glorious photography.

Finally, this book would not have been possible without the cooperation of all our friends at the wineries who graciously contributed their favorite recipes. I wish to thank them all for their generosity.

Table of Contents

Introduction

🍇 Just mention California wine country and
thoughts of warm sunshine, vines heavy with ripen-
ing grapes, and a relaxed lifestyle come to mind.
The small villages throughout the wine country all
have their own personalities, as do the wineries.
From rural, family-run boutique wineries to large,
stately wineries surrounded by a sea of vineyards,
they all have one thing in common, a love for good
food and wine.

This love of food and wine has resulted in an
explosion of cutting-edge ideas that have defined
California cuisine, incorporating the finest of
Europe and Asia, while drawing on the incredible
local and seasonal bounty.

Entertaining is a way of life in wine country.
Whether it is a formal dinner with many courses to
showcase a variety of wines, or just drawing off a
pitcher of new wine from the barrel to go with an
impromptu picnic with neighbors, the desire to
share the best they have to offer has helped shape
the cuisine of California.

In the following pages you will find recipes
offered from the finest wineries of Northern California. Each reflects the personality of the winery it
comes from, whether formal or casual, and all are
delicious. Each one is a taste of wine country.

1996

TURNBULL

Syrah

Napa Valley
Oakville

Produced & Bottled by
Turnbull Wine Cellars   Oakville, CA

TURNBULL WINE CELLARS

Located just south of world-renowned Oakville in the Napa Valley, Turnbull Wine Cellars produces stunning wines of amazing complexity and depth. Proprietor Patrick O'Dell's well-known red wines include Cabernet Sauvignon, Merlot, and Sangiovese, as well as small amounts of Syrah and Zinfandel. A limited amount of elegant Sauvignon Blanc, is a special treat for white wine lovers who visit his tasting room.

ROASTED GINGER QUAIL *with Shiitake Mushrooms & Soba Noodles*

Beverley Wolfe, executive chef for the winery, took time out of her busy schedule to share one of her favorite dishes with us. I hope you enjoy it as much as her many guests have.

3 tablespoons minced fresh ginger

2 tablespoons sesame oil

1 teaspoon Chinese five spice powder

4 quail

Salt and freshly ground black pepper to taste

2 tablespoons vegetable oil

3 stalks lemon grass, pale tender part only, thinly sliced

1 leek, pale part only, thinly sliced

3 cloves garlic, minced

8 ounces shiitake mushrooms, sliced

2 cups corn kernels

$1/3$ cup sake

5 Roma tomatoes, chopped

2 tablespoons chopped fresh basil

2 tablespoons chopped fresh mint

12 ounces soba noodles, cooked in boiling salted water until al dente then drained

Chopped fresh cilantro for garnish

Black sesame seeds for garnish

(recipe continued on next page)

In a small bowl, mix ginger, sesame oil, and Chinese five spice powder into a paste. Rub paste all over the quail. Cover and chill for at least four hours or overnight.

Preheat oven to 400°F. Lightly oil a baking pan large enough to hold the quail. Season quail with salt and pepper and place in prepared baking pan. Roast for about 45 minutes.

In a large skillet, heat oil over medium-high heat. Add lemon grass, leek, and garlic and stir-fry until just tender. Add mushrooms and corn and stir-fry until mushrooms are tender, and liquid has almost evaporated. Stir in sake. Add tomatoes, basil, and mint. Reduce heat to medium and simmer until tomatoes break down a little.

Remove quail to a platter and keep warm. Pour pan juices into sauce and stir to mix. Add cooked soba noodles and simmer until noodles absorb some of the liquid but are still firm. Divide pasta onto 4 plates. Place a quail on top, sprinkle with cilantro and sesame seeds and serve immediately.

Serves 4
Serve with Turnbull Wine Cellars
Syrah

BELVEDERE VINEYARDS
AND WINERY

*In Italian, "belvedere" means "beautiful view,"
which aptly describes the vista from this rustic redwood winery in the Russian River Valley. The
winery was built in 1982, which was the same year
owners Bill and Sally Hambrecht bought their
first piece of vineyard land high atop Bradford
Mountain in Dry Creek Valley. Over the years they
purchased and planted additional estate vineyards in the Dry Creek, Alexander, and Russian
River Valleys in Northern Sonoma County. As
Bill Hambrecht often says, "Our most valuable
asset is our vineyards. Good vineyards are as
valuable as gold to a winery, and Belvedere has
access to some of Sonoma County's best."*

GRILLED ASIAN
PORK TENDERLOIN
with Noodles

*Belvedere's marketing director, English
Knowles, gave us this dish to showcase their
award winning red Zinfandel.*

MARINADE:

1 cup Belvedere Vineyards and Winery Zinfandel

$1/4$ cup soy sauce

2 tablespoons black bean and garlic sauce

1 tablespoon hoisin sauce

1 teaspoon minced fresh ginger

$1/2$ teaspoon freshly ground black pepper

1 (1-pound) pork tenderloin

$1/4$ cup Belvedere Vineyards and Winery Zinfandel

1 tablespoon cornstarch

$1/4$ cup water

12 ounces Chinese noodles or spaghetti, cooked in
    boiling salted water until al dente, then drained

2 scallions, sliced diagonally

In a bowl, whisk together all of the marinade ingredients. Pour marinade into a resealable plastic bag. Add the pork tenderloin, seal, and chill for at least 2 hours or overnight.

Prepare the grill. Remove the pork tenderloin from the marinade and reserve the marinade. Place the pork on hot grill and cook on all sides until internal temperature reaches 140°F. Remove from grill and let rest 10 minutes before carving.

In a saucepan, stir together the reserved marinade and wine. Bring to a simmer over medium heat. In a small bowl, stir together cornstarch and water until blended. Whisk cornstarch mixture into the simmering marinade. Continue whisking until the sauce has thickened slightly. Divide the hot noodles onto 4 plates. Carve the pork into 8 medallions and place on top of noodles. Pour sauce over and top with scallions. Serve immediately.

Serves 4
Serve with Belvedere Vineyards and Winery Zinfandel

BEAULIEU VINEYARD

Beaulieu Vineyard (BV) was founded in 1900 by Georges de Latour, who came from a winegrowing family in Bordeaux. Since its inception, BV has been an historic, important player in the history of California winemaking. Under the guidance of legendary winemaker Andre Techelistcheff, beginning in 1938, BV's famous Georges de Latour Cabernet Sauvignon Private Reserve set the standard for California Cabernet through the rest of the century. Madame de Latour, who ran the company in the 1940s, was a brilliant and outspoken promoter of BV who even had the audacity to show her family's wines in her native France, and won them over. BV has been a major pioneer of the cool Carneros District of Napa, now legendary for fine Pinot Noir and Chardonnay. The winery is now owned by United Distillers & Vintners North America, and current winemaker, Joel Aiken, continues the great tradition, along with a fine sense of innovation, established by Georges de Latour and Andre Techelistcheff.

Sake Marinated
CHILEAN SEA BASS
in Dashi Broth with
Shrimp Dumplings

This is a recipe worthy of your best friends. The dumplings are heavenly and the sea bass sublime. Although a fair amount of preparation is involved, the results are spectacular.

SAKE MARINADE:

$^2/3$ cup soy sauce

$^1/4$ cup mirin

$^1/4$ cup sake

3 tablespoons sugar

1 tablespoon minced fresh ginger

1 teaspoon minced garlic

2 pounds Chilean sea bass, cut into 6 serving pieces

SHRIMP DUMPLINGS:

$1^1/2$ teaspoons sesame oil

$1^1/2$ teaspoons sake

1 teaspoon cornstarch

1 teaspoon sugar

$^1/2$ teaspoon salt

$^1/4$ teaspoon white pepper

(recipe continued on next page)

6 ounces raw shelled shrimp, finely chopped

1/3 cup finely chopped water chestnuts

1 tablespoon minced scallion

1 egg, lightly beaten

1 tablespoon water

24 round wonton wrappers

DASHI BROTH:

4 cups water

1/4 cup dried bonito flakes

4-inch square piece konbu seaweed

2 scallions, thinly sliced diagonally

For the marinade: Whisk together the marinade ingredients in a shallow dish, just large enough to hold the fish in a single layer. Place the fish in the marinade, cover, and chill overnight, turning several times.

For the dumplings: In a bowl, whisk together the sesame oil, sake, cornstarch, sugar, salt, and white pepper and keep whisking until the sugar dissolves. Add the shrimp, water chestnuts, and scallion and gently toss together until evenly mixed.

In a separate small bowl, whisk together the lightly beaten egg and 1 tablespoon water to make an egg wash. Place a wonton wrapper on a lightly floured surface and brush lightly with egg wash.

Place 2 teaspoons of filling in the center of the wrapper. Bring the edges up around the filling to completely enclose the filling. Gently twist the top to seal the dumpling. Slightly flatten the bottom so that the dumpling will stand upright. Place the dumpling on a lightly floured baking sheet. Repeat until all of the filling is used.

For the dashi: In a saucepan, combine water, bonito flakes, and konbu. Bring to a boil over medium-high heat. As soon as the mixture comes to a boil, remove from heat. Let stand for 15 minutes, then strain through a fine sieve. Discard the solids. Set aside the broth.

To assemble the dish: Remove the sea bass from the marinade. Grill or broil until cooked through but still moist inside.

While the fish is cooking, bring a large pot of salted water to a boil. Add the shrimp dumplings to the boiling water and cook until they rise to the top.

Reheat the dashi broth and divide it into 6 large shallow bowls. Place 4 dumplings in each bowl and place a piece of sea bass in each bowl. Sprinkle with sliced scallions and serve immediately.

Serves 6
Serve with Beaulieu Vineyard Carneros Chardonnay

11

BENZIGER FAMILY WINERY

The Benziger Family, producers of Benziger Family, Reserve, and Imagery Wines, believes that the nature of great wine lies in vineyard character, winemaker artistry, and family passion. At Benziger this means farming and vinifying select vineyards to mine the unique character of each, winemaking that combines intuition and artistry with a minimalist philosophy, and passion that is shared by the entire family. In its quest for uniqueness through diversity, each year the family produces over 300 lots of grapes from over 60 ranches in over a dozen appellations.

ASIAN SAUSAGE
with Pasta

Genie Mosey, Benziger's talented chef, looked toward the east for this superb dish to complement their outstanding Pinot Noir.

ASIAN SAUSAGE:

12 ounces ground pork

12 ounces ground turkey

$1/2$ cup finely chopped red bell pepper

$1/2$ cup finely chopped scallions

1 tablespoon minced garlic

1 tablespoon minced fresh ginger

2 tablespoons olive oil, divided

$1/2$ cup fermented black beans

1 tablespoon minced garlic

3 tablespoons finely chopped onion

1 cup chicken stock

$1/2$ cup chopped water chestnuts

1 teaspoon chile oil

1 teaspoon sesame oil

$1/2$ teaspoon sugar

1 pound Chinese noodles or spaghetti, cooked in boiling salted water until al dente, then drained

(recipe continued on next page)

In a large bowl, combine the sausage ingredients and mix well. Cover the sausage and chill overnight.

In a large wok or skillet, heat 1 tablespoon of the olive oil over medium-high heat. Add the black beans and garlic and stir-fry until fragrant. Transfer mixture to a bowl. Heat the remaining olive oil over medium-high heat and add the sausage. Stir-fry until cooked through. Stir in the reserved black bean mixture, chicken stock, water chestnuts, chile oil, sesame oil, and sugar. Add the hot noodles and stir gently until the liquid is absorbed. Divide onto 6 plates and serve immediately.

Serves 6
Serve with Benziger Family Winery
Pinot Noir

BERINGER VINEYARDS

The oldest continually operating winery in the Napa Valley was started in 1876 by Jacob and Frederick Beringer, immigrants from Mainz, Germany. Currently a publicly traded company, owned by thousands of wine-loving shareholders, Beringer Vineyards excels in the production of vineyard designated reds, graceful and supple whites, and lovingly tended, botrytis-affected, late harvest dessert wines.

PANCETTA & NORI-WRAPPED SWORDFISH
on a Wild Mushroom & Green Tea Soba Noodle Stir-Fry

When you have the time to create kitchen alchemy,
try this amazing recipe from Beringer's
Jerry Comfort. It is an outstanding match
for the Beringer Merlot.

SAUCE:

1 cup Beringer Vineyards Howell Mountain Merlot

1 clove of garlic, thinly sliced

4 thin slices of ginger

1 slice pancetta, minced

2 shallots, minced

4 cups veal stock

1 teaspoon minced garlic

1 teaspoon minced fresh ginger

1 teaspoon soy sauce

BABY BOK CHOY:

2 tablespoon butter

1 teaspoon minced garlic

2 baby bok choy, cut in half lengthwise

WILD MUSHROOM AND GREEN TEA SOBA NOODLE STIR-FRY:

2 tablespoons vegetable oil

1/2 teaspoon minced garlic

1/2 teaspoon minced fresh ginger

4 ounces chanterelle mushrooms, thinly sliced

4 ounces enoki mushrooms

4 ounces shiitake mushrooms, stems removed and
   thinly sliced

1 bunch scallions, sliced diagonally into 1/2-inch
   pieces

1 (7-ounce) package green tea flavored soba
   noodles, cooked in boiling water until al dente,
   then drained

Salt and white pepper to taste

PANCETTA AND NORI-WRAPPED SWORDFISH:

1 pound swordfish loin

Salt and freshly ground black pepper to taste

4 sheets of nori

4 thinly sliced pieces of pancetta

2 tablespoons vegetable oil

🌿 Preheat oven to 375°F.

For the sauce: In a small saucepan, combine the wine, sliced garlic, and sliced ginger. Simmer over medium heat until the liquid is reduced to a syrup. Remove from heat and remove and discard the sliced garlic and sliced ginger. Set the reduced wine aside.

In a saucepan, sauté the minced pancetta over medium heat until crisp. Add the shallots and sauté until tender. Add the veal stock and simmer until reduced to 1 cup. Stir in the reserved reduced wine, minced garlic, minced fresh ginger, and soy sauce. Keep warm and set aside.

For the bok choy: In a small skillet, heat the butter over medium-high heat. Add the ginger and stir-fry until fragrant. Add the bok choy and stir-fry until just tender. Keep warm and set aside.

For the wild mushroom stir-fry: In a wok or skillet, heat the vegetable oil over medium-high heat. Add the garlic and ginger and stir-fry until fragrant. Add the mushrooms and stir-fry until tender. Add the scallions and hot noodles and toss until heated through. Season with salt and white pepper. Keep warm and set aside.

For the swordfish: Cut the swordfish into 4 equal rectangles, approximately 3-inches long and 1-inch wide. Season the swordfish with salt and pepper. Carefully wrap the nori around each piece of swordfish and trim off any excess. Wrap the pancetta slices around the swordfish pieces and secure with toothpicks.

In an ovenproof skillet, heat the vegetable oil over medium-high heat. Add the swordfish and sear on all sides. Place skillet in the oven to finish cooking the swordfish for 5 minutes. Remove from oven.

Divide sauce onto 4 plates. Place a bed of the mushroom-noodle mixture on the sauce. Top with a piece of bok choy and swordfish. Serve immediately.

Serves 4
Serve with Beringer Vineyards
Howell Mountain Merlot

Who swills — sins,
Who sips — prays
Theodor Heuss

CARDINALE WINERY

Cardinale Rule: Make grape selection an obsession and gentle winemaking a virtue. Grow fruit of intense vineyard and varietal character from the finest sites in the Mayacamas. Pick only when the fruit is physiologically ripe and balanced in flavor. Hand harvest into small lug boxes, during the cool of the morning. Keep each vineyard separate, in order to know it better. Hand sort all fruit and use only sound, ripe berries. Carefully crack the berries and begin native yeast fermentation. Gently macerate juice and skins for 25 to 35 days to maximize flavor and texture. Use a traditional basket press to deepen mid-palate flavors. Place into 100% new, tight-grained French oak Chateau barrels. Attentively rack wine from barrel to barrel every three months. Age in barrel for 18 to 21 months. Bottle unfiltered. Age in bottle for 12 months before release. Enjoy or bottle age for an additional 5 to 10 years.

CHINESE GRILLED CHICKEN SALAD
with Pickled Red Onions & Somen Noodles

The pickled red onions are a tangy counterpoint to the savory chicken in this colorful salad.

1 tablespoon hoisin sauce

$1/2$ teaspoon Chinese five spice powder

4 skinless, boneless chicken breasts

Salt and freshly ground black pepper to taste

PICKLED RED ONIONS:

$1/2$ red onion, thinly sliced

$1/4$ cup rice vinegar

DRESSING:

$1/3$ cup vegetable oil

$1/4$ cup hoisin sauce

2 tablespoons freshly squeezed lime juice

2 tablespoons sesame oil

2 tablespoons rice vinegar

$1^1/2$ tablespoons sugar

$1/2$ teaspoon salt

(recipe continued on next page)

8 ounces thin somen noodles, cooked in boiling
salted water until al dente, then drained

8 ounces mixed greens

2 carrots, julienned

2 scallions, thinly sliced diagonally

3 tablespoons vegetable oil

8 wonton wrappers, sliced into ribbons

Salt to taste

In a small bowl, blend together hoisin sauce
and Chinese five spice powder. Rub mixture on all
sides of the chicken breasts and let stand for 30
minutes.

For the red onions: In a shallow bowl, toss the
red onions with the vinegar and set aside for 30
minutes. Drain and set aside.

For the dressing: In a bowl, whisk together the
dressing ingredients until smooth. Reserve $1/4$ cup
of the dressing for the salad and set aside.

Add the hot noodles to the dressing in the bowl
and toss until evenly coated. Let cool, tossing occa-
sionally, so that the noodles absorb the dressing
evenly.

In a large bowl, toss the reserved dressing with the salad greens, carrots, and scallions.

Prepare the grill. Season the chicken with salt and pepper. When hot, place the chicken on the grill and grill until cooked through. Transfer chicken to a cutting board and let stand for 5 minutes before carving. Slice the chicken diagonally.

In a small skillet, heat oil over medium-high heat. Add the sliced wontons and sauté until golden brown and crisp. With a slotted spoon, transfer wontons to a paper towel to drain. Sprinkle with salt.

Divide salad greens onto 4 plates. Divide noodles onto the greens. Fan a piece of chicken on top of the noodles. Scatter pickled red onion on top of chicken. Top with crispy wontons.

Serves 4
Serve with Cardinale Winery
Royale

CEDAR MOUNTAIN
WINERY

The creative interests of Linda and Earl Ault came to fruition in 1990, when they established Cedar Mountain Winery and began production of their award-winning wines. True to their belief that quality wines begin with the finest grapes in the vineyard, the Aults specialize in wines from fruit grown locally in the Livermore Valley. In addition to the classic Chardonnays and Bordelais varieties from these vineyards, a small amount of Port grown in the Sierra Foothills is also produced.

CHOPSTIX NOODLE SALAD

Our dear friend and incomparable director of marketing for Cedar Mountain Winery, Sigrid Liang, composed this wonderful and tasty summer salad.

DRESSING:

1/2 cup Cedar Mountain Winery Chardonnay

1/2 cup vegetable oil

1/4 cup soy sauce

1 tablespoon minced fresh ginger

1 tablespoon peanut butter

1 tablespoon sesame oil

1 tablespoon sugar

2 teaspoons dry mustard

8 ounces Chinese noodles or linguine, cooked in boiling salted water until al dente, then drained

2 cups sliced mushrooms

24 snow peas, blanched and cut in half

1 red bell pepper, julienned

4 scallions, thinly sliced

2 carrots, thinly sliced

2 (8-ounce) cans sliced water chestnuts, rinsed and drained

1/4 cup sesame seeds, lightly toasted

(recipe continued on next page)

🍂 **For the dressing:** In a large bowl, whisk together the dressing ingredients.

Toss the hot noodles with the dressing and let cool completely. Add the mushrooms, snow peas, bell pepper, scallions, carrots, and water chestnuts and toss well. Cover and chill for 1 hour. Sprinkle with sesame seeds and serve.

Serves 4 to 6
Serve with Cedar Mountain Winery
Chardonnay

Of beverages,
wine is the most useful,
Of curatives, the tastiest, and
Of foods, the most pleasant.

Plutarch

CHATEAU MONTELENA
ESTABLISHED 1882

THE MONTELENA ESTATE
Cabernet Sauvignon
NAPA VALLEY
1991
GROWN, PRODUCED & ESTATE BOTTLED BY
CHATEAU MONTELENA WINERY, CALISTOGA, CALIFORNIA
ALCOHOL 14.01% BY VOLUME

CHATEAU MONTELENA WINERY

A visit to Chateau Montelena is a must for wine lovers seeking excellence. With thick natural stone walls, which maintain perfect temperature and humidity for aging wine, and the exceptional grapes that come from the Estate Vineyard, Chateau Montelena has earned its reputation as one of California's finest growers. Even the French, for the first time in the history of winemaking, named the Chateau Montelena Chardonnay the world's greatest Chardonnay in 1976.

VIETNAMESE BEEF & NOODLE SOUP

This is a version of "pho," the delicious traditional soup of Vietnam, which is served with accompaniments that each diner adds to taste.

3 pounds beef soup bones

4 quarts water

1 1/2 pounds chuck steak

1 onion, sliced

1/4 cup fish sauce

2 tablespoons sugar

2-inch piece ginger, peeled and sliced

1 teaspoon salt

3 star anise

2 whole cloves

1 pound rice stick noodles

ACCOMPANIMENTS:

1 1/2 cups bean sprouts

1/4 cup chopped cilantro

4 scallions, thinly sliced

2 small hot chiles, seeded and minced

3 tablespoons chopped fresh mint

3 tablespoons chopped fresh Thai basil

2 limes, quartered

Preheat oven to 425°F. Lightly oil a roasting pan.

Place soup bones in prepared roasting pan. Roast for 30 minutes, or until browned all over. Place bones, water, beef, and onion in a large stock pot. Bring to a boil, then reduce heat to medium-low and simmer for 1 hour. Add fish sauce, sugar, ginger, salt, star anise, and cloves and simmer an additional 2 hours. Strain through a colander and return the broth to the pot. When cool enough to handle, separate the meat from the bones and chop coarsely. Return the beef to the pot.

Soak the rice stick noodles in hot water until tender, then drain. Divide noodles into 6 large bowls. Ladle soup and meat into bowls. Serve with the accompaniments.

Serves 6 to 8
Serve with Chateau Montelena Winery
Cabernet Sauvignon

CLOS PEGASE WINERY

Out of a desire to combine ancient traditions with modern technology, Jan Shrem founded Clos Pegase in 1983. His dream, to create a "temple to wine" has resulted in one of the most stunning and dramatic wineries in the Napa Valley. Surrounded by art, and described as "America's first monument to wine as art," Clos Pegase's wines are stylistic and elegant. Their grace does justice to the winery's namesake, Pegasus, the winged horse of Greek mythology whose hooves unleashed the sacred Spring of the muses, which irrigated vines and inspired poets.

SUKIYAKI

The balanced flavors of this dish echo the Japanese philosophy of harmony.

BROTH:

1¹/2 cups water

2 tablespoons bonito flakes

2-inch square piece dried konbu seaweed

1/2 cup mirin

1/3 cup soy sauce

2 tablespoons sugar

1¹/2 tablespoons sake

6 dry shiitake mushrooms

3 tablespoons vegetable oil

1 pound top round steak, thinly sliced across
    the grain

Salt and freshly ground black pepper to taste

1 (14-ounce) package tofu, cut into 1/4-inch cubes

10 ounces Napa cabbage, coarsely chopped

5 ounces fresh spinach, coarsely chopped

1 onion, cut in half then sliced

6 ounces cellophane noodles, soaked in hot water
    until tender, then drained

(recipe continued on next page)

For the broth: In a saucepan, combine water, bonito flakes, and konbu. Bring to a boil over medium-high heat. As soon as the mixture comes to a boil, remove from heat. Let stand for 15 minutes, then strain through a fine sieve into a bowl and discard the solids. Stir in mirin, soy sauce, sugar, and sake. Set aside.

Soak the mushrooms in hot water until tender. Drain and discard soaking liquid. Slice the mushroom caps and discard the tough stems. Set mushroom caps aside.

In a large skillet, heat oil over medium-high heat. Season the sliced beef with salt and pepper. Add to the skillet and stir-fry until lightly browned. Push the beef aside, add the tofu and stir-fry until lightly browned. Add the reserved mushrooms, cabbage, spinach, and onion and stir-fry until the cabbage is wilted. Pour in reserved broth and bring to a simmer. Add the noodles and simmer until the broth is slightly absorbed by the noodles. Divide into large shallow bowls and serve immediately.

Serves 6 to 8
Serve with Clos Pegase Winery
Sauvignon Blanc

DE LOACH
VINEYARDS

The morning fog along the Russian River Valley, a product of marine influence, is instrumental in creating the quality of Cecil and Christine De Loach's estate grown wines. This cooling influence in the heat of late summer allows their vines to fully develop their fruit, while maintaining acidity and elegance. Cecil and Christine De Loach's personal connection to their vineyards and cellar ensures a consistency of style and excellence in quality year after year.

HOT & SOUR SHRIMP
with Rice Noodles

If you like your cuisine a bit more on the hot side, increase the sambal oelek in this flavorful dish.

1/4 cup vegetable oil, divided

1 tablespoon minced garlic

1 tablespoon minced fresh ginger

1 pound medium shelled shrimp

1 onion, cut in half then sliced

1 carrot, julienned

4 ounces snow peas, cut in half

1/2 cup sliced water chestnuts

1 cup chicken stock

1/4 cup soy sauce

1/4 cup rice vinegar

2 tablespoons sake

1 tablespoon sesame oil

1 tablespoon sugar

1 teaspoon sambal oelek or other hot chile paste

8 ounces wide rice noodles, soaked in hot water
     until tender, then drained

1 tablespoon cornstarch

3 tablespoons water

🍃 In a large wok or skillet, heat 2 tablespoons of the oil over high heat. Add the garlic and ginger and stir-fry until fragrant. Add the shrimp and stir-fry just until pink. Transfer shrimp to a bowl and set aside.

Add the remaining oil to the wok. When hot, add the onion and carrot and stir-fry just until tender. Add the snow peas and water chestnuts and stir-fry for 1 minute. Stir in the chicken stock, soy sauce, vinegar, sake, sesame oil, sugar, and sambal oelek and simmer until the liquid is reduced by half. Reduce heat under the wok to medium and add the noodles and reserved shrimp. In a small bowl, stir together the cornstarch and water until smooth. Stir cornstarch mixture into the wok and simmer until slightly thickened. Divide onto 4 plates and serve immediately.

Serves 4
Serve with De Loach Vineyards
Zinfandel

DOMAINE CARNEROS

Designed after Château de la Marquetterie in Champagne, with its roots in the French house of Taittinger, Domaine Carneros is the only sparkling wine producer using exclusively Carneros grapes for their super-premium méthode champenoise. Situated atop a knoll surrounded by its vineyards, the château commands a spectacular view of the rolling hills of Carneros. Pinot Noir and Chardonnay, along with a lesser amount of Pinot Meunier serve as the basis of Domaine Carneros' elegant and delicate sparkling wines.

SCALLOPS & ASPARAGUS
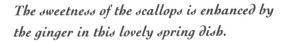
with Ginger & Sesame Somen

The sweetness of the scallops is enhanced by the ginger in this lovely spring dish.

3 tablespoons vegetable oil

1 tablespoon minced fresh ginger

1 clove garlic, minced

1 pound scallops, quartered if large

1 pound asparagus, sliced on the diagonal into 2-inch pieces

$^1/_3$ cup soy sauce

3 tablespoons mirin

2 tablespoons sugar

1 tablespoon sake

1 tablespoon sesame oil

8 ounces somen noodles or spaghetti, cooked in boiling salted water until al dente, then drained

2 tablespoons sesame seeds, lightly toasted

In a skillet, heat the oil over medium-high heat. Add the ginger and garlic and stir-fry until fragrant. Add the scallops and stir-fry until lightly browned. With a slotted spoon, transfer scallops to a bowl and set aside.

(recipe continued on next page)

Add the asparagus, soy sauce, mirin, sugar, sake, and sesame oil to the skillet and bring to a simmer. Simmer until the asparagus is crisp-tender. Stir in the somen and simmer until the noodles have absorbed most of the liquid. Return the scallops, and any accumulated juices, to the skillet. Toss to coat and simmer until the liquid has almost evaporated. Divide onto 6 plates and sprinkle with sesame seeds. Serve immediately.

Serves 6
Serve with Domaine Carneros
Le Rêve Sparkling Wine

I rather like bad wine...one gets so bored with good wine.
Disraeli

DUCKHORN VINEYARDS

When your last name is Duckhorn, it stands to reason that you would choose a duck to be the symbol for your winery. Dan and Margaret Duckhorn have taken that theme and created one of the Napa Valley's most respected premium wineries. Hand-harvested and sorted grapes enter their crusher to emerge as ultra-premium Cabernets, Merlots, Zinfandels, and Sauvignon Blancs. New vineyards in Mendocino's Anderson Valley promise to deliver world-class Pinot Noirs to their flock of stylistic wines.

BRAISED BEEF *with Star Anise & Orange Sauce over Wide Noodles*

Wait until the chill of winter sets in to serve this rich and hearty dish to your family and friends.

2 pounds top round, sliced across the grain $1/4$-inch wide and 4 inches long

1 tablespoon cornstarch

$1/4$ cup vegetable oil, divided

2 scallions, chopped

1 tablespoon minced fresh ginger

4 cloves garlic, minced

$3/4$ cup freshly squeezed orange juice

$3/4$ cup water

$1/2$ cup soy sauce

$1/4$ cup hoisin sauce

$1/4$ cup sake

Zest of 1 orange, finely minced

3 whole star anise

1 pound wide egg noodles, cooked in boiling salted water until al dente, then drained

🍃 In a bowl, combine beef with cornstarch and 1 tablespoon of the oil and mix until evenly coated. Let marinate 30 minutes.

In a large skillet, heat the remaining 3 tablespoons oil over medium-high heat. Add the scallions, ginger, and garlic and stir-fry until fragrant. Add the beef and stir-fry until lightly browned. Stir in orange juice, water, soy sauce, hoisin sauce, sake, orange zest, and star anise and bring to a simmer. Reduce heat to medium-low, cover skillet, and simmer for about 1 hour, or until the meat is very tender. If the sauce is not thick enough, remove the cover of the skillet and simmer until slightly thickened. Serve over hot pasta.

Serves 6
Serve with Duckhorn Vineyards
Estate Grown Merlot

DRY CREEK VINEYARD

Dry Creek Vineyard was the first new winery to be established in the Dry Creek Valley of Sonoma after Prohibition. Synonymous with fine winemaking, Dry Creek Vineyard draws upon over 35 different vineyards to produce their wines, matching the particular soils and microclimates of each site to the varieties that do best.

POTSTICKERS

I have been on a quest for the perfect potsticker and this is it. They freeze beautifully, so keep some on hand for unexpected guests.

DIPPING SAUCE:

1/4 cup soy sauce

1/4 cup rice vinegar

3 scallions, minced

2 cloves garlic, minced

1 teaspoon sesame oil

1 teaspoon sugar

1/4 teaspoon dried hot red chile flakes

POTSTICKERS:

3 scallions, minced

3 tablespoons soy sauce

2 tablespoons sesame oil

1 tablespoon sake

1 1/2 teaspoons minced fresh ginger

1 teaspoon salt

1/2 teaspoon pepper

1 egg

1 pound cabbage, chopped

1 pound ground pork

(recipe continued on next page)

1 egg, lightly beaten

1 tablespoon water

Round wonton wrappers

1/4 cup vegetable oil

Water

For the dipping sauce: In a bowl, whisk all ingredients together until sugar dissolves. Cover and let sit at room temperature for 30 minutes to allow the flavors to marry.

For the potstickers: In a large bowl, stir together scallions, soy sauce, sesame oil, sake, ginger, salt, and pepper. Add the egg and whisk until blended. Place chopped cabbage in the bowl of a food processor and process until finely chopped. Add cabbage and pork to the seasoning in the bowl and mix until well blended.

In a small bowl, whisk together lightly beaten egg and 1 tablespoon water to make an egg wash. Place wonton wrappers on a lightly floured surface and brush each lightly with egg wash. Place a tablespoon of filling in the center of the wrapper and fold over to make a half moon shape. Pinch the top together at midpoint. Working from the edge, pleat the dough towards the center, making 3 pleats on each side so the potsticker will be completely sealed. Slightly flatten the bottom so that the potsticker will stand upright. Place the potsticker, pleated edge up, on a lightly floured baking sheet. Repeat until all of the filling is used.

In a large nonstick skillet, heat the oil over medium-high heat. Arrange the potstickers in the skillet in a closely packed circle, pleated sides up. Cook until the edges begin to brown. Add enough water to come halfway up the sides of the potstickers. Take care since the oil will splatter a bit. Cover the skillet and reduce the heat to medium. Cook for 6 to 8 minutes to steam the potstickers. Remove the lid and continue to cook until all the liquid has evaporated and the potstickers begin to sizzle in the remaining oil. When the bottoms are well browned and crisp, transfer to a serving plate. Divide the dipping sauce into small individual bowls. Serve immediately.

These freeze beautifully. When cooking frozen potstickers, place in the skillet directly from the freezer, cook according to the directions but steam them for 10 minutes.

Makes about 80
Serve with Dry Creek Vineyard
Merlot

FERRARI-CARANO
VINEYARDS AND WINERY

Villa Fiore, or "House of Flowers," at Ferrari-Carano is one of the most spectacular wineries and visitors' centers in the northern California wine country. Designed to reflect the proud Italian heritage of the Carano family, Villa Fiore houses state-of-the art kitchens, which are used to educate professionals as well as consumers in the enjoyment of Ferrari-Carano wines.

Ferrari-Carano draws its grapes from fourteen winery-owned vineyards over a fifty-mile area from Alexander Valley in the north to the Carneros district in the south. This exceptional supply of fruit allows the winemaker to produce the highly stylized wines for which Ferrari-Carano is known.

ORIENTAL PASTA SALAD
with Peanut Sesame Sauce

The hot days of wine country summer call for cooling and light salads. Try this with chilled Ferrari-Carano Fumé Blanc.

1 pound Chinese noodles or spaghetti, cooked in boiling salted water until al dente, then drained

2 tablespoons vegetable oil

1 carrot, grated

1 jicama, peeled and julienned

3 scallions, thinly sliced

1/2 cup roasted peanuts, coarsely chopped

DRESSING:

1/3 cup peanut butter

1/3 cup soy sauce

1/3 cup tahini

1/3 cup vegetable oil

1/4 cup chicken stock

1/4 cup honey

1/4 cup rice vinegar

2 tablespoons sesame oil

2 teaspoons minced fresh ginger

4 cloves garlic, minced

(recipe continued on next page)

In a large bowl, toss hot cooked pasta with 2 tablespoons vegetable oil. Set aside until cool. Add carrot, jicama, scallions, and peanuts and toss gently.

For the dressing: Combine peanut butter, soy sauce, tahini, vegetable oil, chicken stock, honey, rice vinegar, sesame oil, ginger, and garlic in a blender and blend until smooth. Pour dressing over pasta and toss gently but thoroughly. Serve chilled or at room temperature.

Serves 4 to 6
Serve with Ferrari-Carano Vineyards
Fumé Blanc Reserve

And Noah he often said
to his wife when he sat down to dine,
"I don't care where the water goes if it
doesn't get into the wine."
Chesterton

GEYSER PEAK WINERY

Located just north of Healdsburg, 100-year-old Geyser Peak Winery's tradition of excellence shows in their being named "1998 Winery of the Year" by Wine & Spirits Magazine *and the San Francisco International Wine Competition. Their original vine-covered stone winery is now the cornerstone of a state-of-the-art complex that is one of the most well equipped wineries in California. Within the winery, president and head winemaker Daryl Groom oversees the vinification of not only their sought-after reserve wines but also a multitude of great wines for all occasions.*

BAKED RICE STICK NOODLES *with Shrimp & Snow Peas*

This is a nice dish to pull out of the oven when your family comes home on a cool, autumn afternoon.

1 tablespoon vegetable oil

1 onion, chopped

1 tablespoon minced garlic

1 tablespoon minced fresh ginger

1 tablespoon minced lemon grass, pale tender part only

1/4 cup beef stock

1/4 cup chopped cilantro

3 tablespoons soy sauce

2 tablespoons oyster sauce

1 teaspoon minced fresh hot green chile

8 ounces rice stick noodles

1 teaspoon sesame oil

1 pound shelled medium shrimp, cut in half

8 ounces snow peas, cut in half

Preheat oven to 350°F. Lightly oil a 2-quart baking dish with a lid.

In a skillet, heat the oil over medium heat. Add the onion and garlic and sauté until the onion is tender. Stir in the ginger and lemon grass and sauté until fragrant. Transfer to a large bowl. Add beef stock, cilantro, soy sauce, oyster sauce, and chile and mix well.

Soak rice stick noodles in hot water until just tender. Drain and toss with sesame oil. Add the noodles, shrimp, and snow peas to the bowl with the onion mixture and toss to mix well. Pour mixture into the prepared baking dish and cover. Bake for 30 minutes, or until hot and bubbly. Serve immediately.

Serves 4 to 6
Serve with Geyser Peak Winery
Shiraz

GLEN ELLEN WINERY

Glen Ellen Winery was created in 1983 by the Benziger family with the idea of producing inexpensive and delicious varietal wines for an increasing number of wine consumers. Thus was born the whole category of "fighting varietals." The winery is located in Sonoma, California, with a wonderful Visitors' Center located in the charming town of Glen Ellen in the historic Valley of the Moon, Sonoma County. In 1994, the Benzigers sold the winery to United Distillers and Vintners (UDV). UDV continues to produce Glen Ellen Proprietor's Reserve wines with the same degree of dedication to quality; not surprising, as the winemaking team has remained virtually unchanged for nearly a decade. Glen Ellen utilizes an innovative program, the Grower Feedback Loop, to encourage their many growers to improve the quality of the fruit produced each year to meet consumers' growing sophistication.

CALAMARI STUFFED *with* PORK
& Cellophane Noodles with a Spicy Dipping Sauce

This impressive dish can be put together well in advance of your dinner party.

SPICY DIPPING SAUCE:

2 tablespoons fish sauce

2 tablespoons freshly squeezed lime juice

2 tablespoons rice vinegar

2 tablespoons water

1 tablespoon sugar

2 teaspoons minced garlic

$1/2$ teaspoon sambal oelek or other hot chile paste

4 dried shiitake mushrooms

6 ounces ground pork

$1^1/2$ ounces thin cellophane noodles, soaked in hot water until tender, then drained and chopped

3 tablespoons finely chopped water chestnuts

2 scallions, chopped

1 tablespoon minced fresh mint

1 tablespoon minced fresh Thai basil

1 tablespoon soy sauce

(recipe continued on next page)

1 tablespoon rice vinegar

2 teaspoons minced fresh ginger

1 teaspoon minced garlic

1 teaspoon fish sauce

1 pound, 8 ounces small to medium-sized calamari, cleaned with tentacles reserved for another use

2 tablespoons vegetable oil

1/2 cup chicken stock

6 ounces mixed greens

For the dipping sauce: In a bowl, whisk together the dipping sauce ingredients and set aside.

Soak the shiitake mushrooms in hot water until tender. Chop the mushrooms and discard the tough stems.

In the bowl of a food processor, combine the chopped mushrooms, pork, chopped cellophane noodles, water chestnuts, scallions, mint, basil, soy sauce, vinegar, ginger, garlic, and fish sauce. Pulse, scraping sides often, until finely chopped and well blended.

Using a small spoon and your fingers, stuff the calamari bodies two-thirds full with the filling. Secure the openings with toothpicks. Prick the calamari with a small sharp knife several times to allow steam to escape during cooking.

In a skillet large enough to hold the stuffed calamari in a single layer, heat the oil over medium heat. Place the calamari in the skillet and lightly brown. Pour in the chicken stock, cover the skillet, and cook for an additional 10 minutes.

Divide the greens onto 6 plates. Divide the dipping sauce into 6 small individual dishes. Place the calamari on the greens and serve immediately.

Serves 6
Serve with Glen Ellen Winery
Pinot Noir

I drank at every vine.
The last was like the first.
I came upon no wine
As wonderful as thirst.

Millay

GLORIA FERRER
CHAMPAGNE CAVES

Founded by José Ferrer, son of Pedro Ferrer Bosch, the Spanish-Catalan founder of Freixenet, Gloria Ferrer Champagne Caves was opened to the public in July of 1986. Named for José Ferrer's beloved wife, Gloria, the winery has been winning awards and accolades of wine critics ever since. Located within the cool Carneros appellation, Gloria Ferrer's beautiful winery with its stucco walls, arched windows, and overhanging balconies is a piece of the proud history of old Spain.

THAI RED CURRIED SCALLOPS
with Wide Noodles

This is proof positive that sparkling wine goes with all foods. Serve this at your next gathering.

12 ounces wide rice stick noodles

$1/2$ teaspoon sesame oil

2 tablespoons vegetable oil, divided

2 tablespoons minced shallots

2 cloves garlic, minced

1 pound scallops

6 scallions, thinly sliced

1 tablespoon minced lemon grass, pale tender part only

1 tablespoon red curry paste

1 (13-ounce) can coconut milk

1 tablespoon fish sauce

(recipe continued on next page)

Soak the noodles in hot water for 15 minutes, or until tender, then drain. Toss with sesame oil and set aside.

In a large wok or skillet, heat 1 tablespoon of the oil over high heat. Add the shallots and garlic and stir-fry until fragrant. Add the scallops and stir-fry until seared on all sides. Transfer scallops to a bowl.

Heat remaining oil in the wok and add the scallions and lemon grass and stir-fry until fragrant. Stir in the red curry paste and stir-fry for 1 minute. Whisk in the coconut milk and fish sauce until blended. Reduce the heat to medium and add the reserved noodles and reserved scallops. Simmer until heated through and slightly thickened. Divide onto 4 plates and serve immediately.

Serves 4
Serve with Gloria Ferrer Champagne Caves
Blanc de Noirs

Napa Valley
FUMÉ BLANC
Dry Sauvignon Blanc
1996

PRODUCED AND BOTTLED BY GRGICH HILLS CELLAR
RUTHERFORD, CA · ALC. 12.8% BY VOL. · CONTAINS SULFITES

GRGICH HILLS CELLAR

Grgich Hills Cellar, a collaboration between Miljenko Grgich and Austin Hills of the Hills Bros. Coffee family, has become known as the producer of big, mouth-filling Chardonnays, which connoisseurs consider to be among the finest of the world.

In addition to their incomparable Chardonnays, Grgich Hills produces a lush and firm Cabernet Sauvignon from estate vineyards in Yountville, as well as a delightfully clean and fruity Fumé Blanc from their Olive Hills estate vineyard. Of particular interest are their dry-land farmed Zinfandels, grown on hot and windy hillside vineyard sites. These massive wines have impressive fruit and longevity.

SINGAPORE NOODLES *with* Chinese Barbequed Pork

This dish will transport you to the exotic night markets in Singapore.

1/4 cup vegetable oil

3 shallots, thinly sliced into rings

5 ounces fresh spinach, chopped

2 cloves garlic, minced

2 teaspoons minced fresh ginger

2 tablespoons oyster sauce

2 tablespoons soy sauce

1 tablespoon sesame oil

2 teaspoons sambal oelek or other hot chile paste

1 teaspoon sugar

8 ounces rice noodles, soaked in hot water until tender, then drained

8 ounces Chinese barbequed pork, sliced

In a large wok or skillet, heat oil over medium heat. Add the shallots and stir-fry until golden brown and crispy. With a slotted spoon, transfer shallots to a paper towel to drain. Set aside.

Add the spinach to the wok and stir-fry until wilted. Add the garlic and ginger and stir-fry until fragrant. Add the oyster sauce, soy sauce, sesame oil, sambal oelek, and sugar and stir until sugar dissolves. Add the hot noodles and simmer until all of the liquid has been absorbed.

Divide the noodle mixture onto 4 plates. Top with barbequed pork. Scatter the crispy shallots over and serve immediately.

Serves 4
Serve with Grgich Hills Cellar
Fumé Blanc

KENDALL-JACKSON WINERY

In 1974, Jess Jackson and his family purchased an 85-acre pear ranch near Lakeport, in Northern California. By 1982 the ranch was a vineyard, the barn was a tasting room, and the pasture was a winery. Meanwhile, the Jackson Family studied the premium vineyards that span California's cool coastal growing regions and discovered the wonderful spectrum of flavors produced by the same grape varietal grown in different locations. They asked themselves, "Why not use this exciting diversity? Why not blend the best grapes from the best vineyards to produce unique wines with layers of depth and complexity?"

Their first Chardonnay was made in 1982 from vineyards in Santa Barbara, Monterey, Sonoma, and Lake Counties. This wine was named "Best American Chardonnay" by the American Wine Competition. Their concept of blending the best with the best was affirmed and to this day continues to be the reason their wines are noted for their consistency and complexity, vintage after vintage.

PAD THAI

*This is one of the best versions of Thailand's
national noodle dish. It is sure to become
the one by which you measure all others.*

PAD THAI SAUCE:

1/3 cup hot water

1 tablespoon dried tamarind

1/2 cup fish sauce

1/2 cup ketchup

1/3 cup lightly packed chopped cilantro

1/4 cup freshly squeezed lime juice

1/4 cup sugar

1/4 cup water

1 tablespoon dried red chile flakes, or to taste

1 tablespoon paprika

12 ounces rice noodles

2 tablespoons sesame oil

1/3 cup vegetable oil, divided

1 onion, chopped

6 cloves garlic, minced

1 cup bean sprouts, cut in half

2 eggs, beaten

(recipe continued on next page)

2 skinless, boneless chicken breasts, cubed

8 ounces medium raw shrimp, shelled and
   deveined

1 cup diced extra-firm tofu

3/4 cup finely chopped peanuts, for garnish

1/2 cup bean sprouts, cut in half, for garnish

6 scallions, chopped, for garnish

For the pad Thai sauce: In a small bowl,
combine hot water and tamarind. Let stand 30 minutes then strain. Reserve liquid and discard solids.
In a large bowl, combine tamarind liquid with
remaining sauce ingredients. Mix well and set
aside.

Soak the rice noodles in cold water for 30 minutes, or until soft. Drain well and toss with sesame
oil until well coated. Set aside.

In a large wok or skillet, heat 3 tablespoons of
the oil over medium-high heat. Add onion and garlic and stir-fry until onion is translucent. Add bean
sprouts and stir-fry until liquid evaporates but
sprouts are still crunchy. Push vegetables aside and
pour in the beaten eggs. Cook until set, then slice
into ribbons and lightly stir into the vegetables.
Transfer cooked vegetable mixture to a bowl and
set aside.

Add 2 tablespoons of the oil to the skillet and add chicken. Stir-fry until golden. Add shrimp and stir-fry until just pink. Push meat aside and add tofu. Stir-fry until golden. Transfer to the bowl with the cooked vegetables and set aside.

Add 1 tablespoon oil into skillet and add rice noodles. Stir-fry about 3 minutes. Add reserved pad Thai sauce and simmer, stirring often, until sauce starts to be absorbed by the noodles. Add reserved vegetables and meat mixture and stir gently until mixture is well coated. Simmer until heated through and most of the liquid has evaporated. Garnish with peanuts, bean sprouts and scallions.

Serves 6 to 8
Serve with Kendall-Jackson Winery Chardonnay

KENWOOD VINEYARDS

At Kenwood Vineyards each vineyard lot is handled separately within the winery to preserve its individuality. Such "small lot" winemaking allows the winemaker to bring each lot of wine to its fullest potential. This style of winemaking is evident in the quality of Kenwood's special bottlings. From the Jack London Vineyard series, whose grapes come from the historical, lava-terraced vineyards of the Jack London Ranch, to the Artist Series Cabernet Sauvignon, whose labels each year feature the work of a renowned artist, Kenwood's reds show Sonoma at its best.

CAPELLINI *with Marinated Sea Scallops & Rock Shrimp with Wasabi Sauce*

Linda Kittler, the Kenwood Vineyards executive chef, devised this subtle and exquisite dish to go with their outstanding Sauvignon Blanc.

MARINADE:

1 1/2 cups Kenwood Vineyards Sonoma Valley Chardonnay

1/2 cup soy sauce

8 ounces sea scallops, quartered

8 ounces rock shrimp, cut in half

WASABI SAUCE:

7 tablespoons vegetable oil, divided

1 tablespoon thinly sliced garlic

1 tablespoon thinly sliced ginger

3/4 cup thinly sliced scallions

1/2 cup sliced snow peas

1/3 cup sliced water chestnuts

4 large fresh shiitake mushrooms, stems discarded and sliced

2 cups Kenwood Vineyards Sauvignon Blanc

(recipe continued on next page)

2 cups chicken stock

1 tablespoon cornstarch

1 tablespoon water

1 1/2 tablespoons wasabi powder

1 1/2 tablespoons water

1/2 teaspoon minced lime zest

Salt to taste

12 ounces capellini, cooked in boiling salted
water until al dente, then drained

For the marinade: In a bowl, stir together
Chardonnay and soy sauce. Add scallops and
shrimp and marinate 30 minutes. Drain and set
aside seafood. Discard marinade.

For the wasabi sauce: In a large wok or skillet,
heat 3 tablespoons of the oil over high heat. Add
garlic and ginger and stir-fry until fragrant. Add
scallions, snow peas, and water chestnuts and stir-
fry until barely tender. Transfer vegetable mixture
to a bowl. Add 2 tablespoons of oil to the wok and,
when hot, add reserved scallops and shrimp and
stir-fry just until cooked. Transfer with a slotted
spoon to vegetable mixture. Add remaining 2 tablespoons oil to the wok and, when hot, add mushrooms and stir-fry until tender. Pour in Sauvignon
Blanc, reduce heat to medium-high, and simmer

until liquid is reduced by half. Add chicken stock and simmer until liquid is reduced by half. In a small bowl, stir together cornstarch and 1 tablespoon water until smooth. Whisk into sauce and simmer until slightly thickened. In a small bowl stir together wasabi and 1 1/2 tablespoons water until smooth. Whisk into sauce. Stir in lime zest, reserved vegetables, and seafood and season with salt. Simmer until heated through and serve over hot pasta.

Serves 4
Serve with Kenwood Vineyards
Sauvignon Blanc

Fill high the bowl
with Samian wine!
Byron

KORBEL CHAMPAGNE
CELLARS

Located just east of Guerneville and just a handful of miles inland from the Pacific Ocean, Korbel Champagne Cellars has stood for fine méthode champenoise sparkling wines for over a hundred years. Founded in the late 1880s by three immigrant brothers from Bohemia, Francis, Anton and Joseph Korbel, and owned and managed by the Heck family since 1954, Korbel has developed into one of California's most respected champagne houses.

SPICY STIR-FRIED NOODLES *with Shrimp & Chinese Sausage*

The slight sweetness of the Chinese sausage enhances the bright flavors of the ginger and chiles.

1/4 cup soy sauce

2 tablespoons fish sauce

1 tablespoon sugar

2 teaspoons sambal oelek or other hot chile paste

3 tablespoons vegetable oil

2 shallots, finely chopped

1 tablespoon minced fresh ginger

8 ounces large raw shelled shrimp, cut in half lengthwise

3 Chinese sausages, thinly sliced on the diagonal

2 eggs, lightly beaten

8 ounces wide egg noodles, cooked in boiling salted water until al dente, then drained

4 ounces bean sprouts

2 scallions, thinly sliced on the diagonal

(recipe continued on next page)

In a small bowl, whisk together the soy sauce, fish sauce, sugar, and sambal oelek until the sugar dissolves. Set aside.

In a large skillet, heat the oil over medium-high heat. Add the shallots and ginger and stir-fry until fragrant. Add the shrimp and Chinese sausages and stir-fry until the shrimp are cooked. Push aside the shrimp and sausages and pour the eggs into the skillet. Cook until the eggs are set, then slice into ribbons with the edge of a spatula. Add the noodles and stir-fry until the ingredients are well mixed. Pour in the reserved soy sauce mixture and bring to a simmer. Continue to cook until the liquid is almost evaporated. Stir in the bean sprouts and scallions and cook until the bean sprouts are crisp-tender. Divide onto plates and serve immediately.

Serves 6
Serve with Korbel Champagne Cellars
Chardonnay Champagne

LEDSON VINEYARDS
AND WINERY

*One of Northern California's newest wineries,
Ledson is rapidly making a name for itself with its
reserve Merlots, floral and fruity Rieslings, and
intense Chardonnays. Located in Sonoma County's
Valley of the Moon, Ledson is at home in a fantas-
tic brick and mortar gothic-style mansion known
affectionately as "The Castle." Two full-time chefs
guarantee Ledson's commitment to the art and cul-
ture of pairing food and great wine.*

CHOP CHAE

This version of one of Korea's national dishes is a natural for the floral aromas of Ledson's Riesling.

MARINADE:

1 tablespoon minced scallions

1 tablespoon sesame seeds

1 tablespoon soy sauce

1 tablespoon sugar

1 teaspoon minced garlic

1 teaspoon sesame oil

12 ounces flank steak, thinly sliced across the grain

SAUCE:

$1/4$ cup soy sauce

2 tablespoons minced scallions

2 tablespoons sugar

1 tablespoon sesame seeds

2 teaspoons minced garlic

$1/2$ teaspoon freshly ground black pepper

$1/2$ cup vegetable oil, divided

1 carrot, julienned

1 cup thinly sliced onion

4 ounces mushrooms, thinly sliced

4 ounces bean sprouts

1 cup julienned cucumber

6 ounces cellophane noodles, soaked in hot water until tender, then drained

For the marinade: In a bowl, stir together the marinade ingredients. Add the sliced beef and mix well. Let marinate for 30 minutes.

For the sauce: In a small bowl, stir the sauce ingredients together and set aside.

In a large skillet, heat 2 tablespoons of the oil over high heat. Add the beef to the skillet and stir-fry until lightly browned. Transfer to a bowl. Add 2 tablespoons of the oil to the skillet and add the carrot and onion. Stir-fry until lightly browned then transfer to the bowl with the beef. Add 2 tablespoons of the oil to the skillet and add the mushrooms. Stir-fry until lightly browned then add to bowl with the beef mixture. Add 1 tablespoon of the oil to the skillet and add the bean sprouts and cucumber. Stir-fry just until barely wilted then add to the beef mixture. Add the remaining 1 tablespoon of oil to the skillet and add the cellophane noodles and reserved sauce mixture. Stir-fry until the noodles begin to absorb the sauce. Return the beef and vegetables to the skillet and stir-fry until most of the sauce has been absorbed. Divide onto 4 plates and serve immediately.

Serves 4
Serve with Ledson Vineyards and Winery
Monterey Johannisberg Riesling

GEWÜRZTRAMINER
RUSSIAN RIVER VALLEY
VINTAGE 1996

MARK WEST ESTATE
VINEYARD AND WINERY

Certified organic since 1990, Mark West Estate Vineyard and Winery is located where the cooling effects of the nearby Pacific Ocean and the fogs of San Pablo Bay provide ideal growing conditions for their fruit. Their 66 acres of Chardonnay, Pinot Noir, Gewürztraminer, and Merlot, whose original plantings date back to 1974, show restrained elegance and delicate, yet multilayered fruit. Ideal to show off the nuances of a subtly seasoned cuisine, the wines of Mark West are proof positive that wine enhances a fine meal.

CHICKEN & BUCKWHEAT SOBA SALAD

This recipe, created by chefs Barbara Hom and Patrick Paull, calls for "furikake" which is a Japanese table condiment consisting of dried bonito flakes, dried seaweed, and sesame seeds. It can be found at Asian or Japanese markets.

ASIAN VINAIGRETTE:

2 tablespoons tahini

2 tablespoons grated ginger

2 tablespoons sherry vinegar

1 tablespoon finely minced shallot

1 tablespoon brown sugar

$1/3$ cup olive oil

Salt and white pepper to taste

8 ounces buckwheat soba noodles, cooked in boiling salted water until al dente, then drained

2 tablespoons sesame oil

4 carrots, julienned

6 ounces snow peas, cut in half

2 tablespoons peanut oil

2 skinless, boneless chicken breasts, thinly sliced

2 scallions, cut into 1-inch pieces

4 tablespoons furikake

(recipe continued on next page)

For the Asian vinaigrette: In a bowl, whisk together tahini, ginger, vinegar, shallot, and brown sugar until blended. Whisk in olive oil and season with salt and white pepper. Set aside.

In a large bowl, toss hot noodles with sesame oil until noodles are coated. Cover and set aside to chill.

Blanch carrots in boiling water for 1 minute then drain, cover, and chill.

Blanch snow peas in boiling water for 1 minute then drain, cover, and chill.

In a skillet, heat peanut oil over medium heat. Add chicken and sauté until cooked through. Set aside to cool.

Divide vinaigrette in half and toss with noodles. Divide noodles onto 4 plates. Divide remaining vinaigrette in half and toss half with carrots and snow peas and place on noodles. Toss remaining vinaigrette with chicken and divide onto vegetables. Sprinkle with scallions and furikake and serve.

Serves 4
Serve with Mark West Estate Vineyard and Winery
Russian River Valley Gewürztraminer

MARTINI AND PRATI
WINERY

One of the oldest family-owned wineries in California, Martini and Prati's history goes back to the turn of the century when Rafael Martini settled in the Russian River Valley north of Sebastopol. A winegrower from Italy, Rafael Martini quickly felt at home in Sonoma County, which reminded him with its gentle climate and hills of his native Tuscany. He purchased the Twin Fir Winery, which had been built in 1881, renamed it the R. Martini Wine Company, and began a tradition that still exists today.

GINGER NOODLE SALAD

Chef Barbara Hom, from Night Owl Catering, created this spicy and flavorful salad to balance the heat of a hot summer day.

DRESSING:

1/4 cup red wine vinegar

1/4 cup minced scallions

2 tablespoons minced fresh cilantro

2 tablespoons minced fresh ginger

1 tablespoon minced orange zest

1 clove garlic, minced

2 tablespoons sesame oil

2 tablespoons soy sauce

1 1/2 tablespoons sugar

1 tablespoon sambal oelek or other hot chile paste

1/2 teaspoon crushed Szechuan peppercorns

1 pound Chinese noodles, cooked in boiling salted water until al dente, then drained

2 tablespoons vegetable oil

1 carrot, julienned

1 cup bean sprouts, cut in half

1/2 cucumber, peeled, seeded, and julienned

4 ounces fully-cooked ham, julienned

🍃 **For the dressing:** In a bowl, whisk together all dressing ingredients. Set aside.

Pour hot noodles and vegetable oil into a large bowl and toss to coat well.

Blanch the carrots for 1 minute then drain. Add carrots, bean sprouts, cucumber, and ham to the noodles. Pour dressing over and toss to combine.

Serves 6
Serve with Martini and Prati Winery
Pinot Bianco

A meal without wine is like a day without sunshine.

Brillat-Savarin

MUMM CUVEÉ NAPA

Journey through the vineyards along the peaceful Silverado Trail and come for a visit. You'll see why we chose this glorious place for our home.

Imagine yourself on a terrace, seated under the cool shade of an elegant umbrella. The sun is setting over the Mayacamas mountains in the distance with soft amber and purple hues settling over the hills and vineyards. These images are reflected in your hand by a flute of America's finest sparkling wine—Mumm Cuveé Napa.

VIETNAMESE CELLOPHANE NOODLE SALAD
with Grilled Shrimp

I first enjoyed this salad at a little Vietnamese restaurant in Paris while attending cooking school at the Hotel Ritz. I hope you have as much pleasure with it as I have.

DRESSING:

1/3 cup vegetable oil

1/4 cup rice vinegar

1/4 cup chopped cilantro

3 tablespoons fish sauce

1 tablespoon freshly squeezed lime juice

1 tablespoon sesame oil

1 tablespoon sugar

1 large shallot, minced

1 1/2 teaspoons minced fresh mint

1 teaspoon minced garlic

1 or 2 fresh Thai chiles (or other small hot chiles), minced

1/4 teaspoon white pepper

12 ounces cellophane noodles, soaked in hot water until tender, then drained

(recipe continued on next page)

4 ounces fresh spinach, washed well and chopped

2 tomatoes, diced

1 mango, peeled and diced

1 small red onion, thinly sliced

1 small red bell pepper, thinly sliced

1 pound large raw shrimp, peeled with tails left on

Vegetable oil

In a large serving bowl, whisk together all dressing ingredients until blended. Add noodles to the dressing and stir to coat. Add spinach, tomatoes, mango, red onion, and red pepper and toss well.

Prepare grill. Brush shrimp with oil and grill until pink. Add to noodles and toss well. Serve at room temperature or chilled.

Serves 4 to 6
Serve with Mumm Cuveé Napa
Brût Prestige

NAVARRO VINEYARDS

Hardly another winery in Northern California has had as much success with its wines as Navarro Vineyards. Visitors to this winery's tasting room, when asking about one of the current vintages, are often regretfully informed, "Sorry, the Chardonnay and Pinot Noir have sold out." This speaks for the absolute quality standards that Ted Bennet and Deborah Cahn have set for the wines they make.

Known for their incredible delicacy and fruit, Navarro's wines are not just your standard California varietals. In addition to their outstanding Pinot Noir and Chardonnay, they take great pains to keep other, lesser-known wines in production. Their Chenin Blanc, White Riesling, and Gewürztraminers are known to wine lovers as among the world's finest, and their Sauvignon Blanc, Pinot Gris, Muscat Blanc, and Valdiguié, never fail to charm first-time tasters.

THAI PESTO

The tangy bite of the lemon grass and the exotic flavors of chile and fish sauce give this variation of a European classic an unusual twist.

1/2 cup lightly packed cilantro leaves

1/2 cup lightly packed Thai basil leaves

1 scallion, chopped

2 cloves garlic, chopped

1 tablespoon minced lemon grass, pale tender part only

1 tablespoon freshly squeezed lime juice

1 tablespoon sweet chile sauce

2 teaspoons fish sauce

1 teaspoon sesame oil

1/4 cup vegetable oil

12 ounces spaghetti, cooked in boiling salted water until al dente, then drained

In the bowl of a food processor, combine cilantro, basil, scallion, garlic, lemon grass, lime juice, chile sauce, fish sauce, and sesame oil and process until smooth. With the motor running, add the vegetable oil in a thin stream until incorporated. Toss with the hot pasta and serve immediately.

Serves 4 to 6
Serve with Navarro Vineyards
Pinot Noir

Good wine is a good familiar creature if it be well used.

Shakespeare

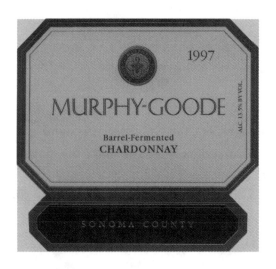

MURPHY-GOODE ESTATE WINERY

Grape growers Tim Murphy and Dale Goode teamed up with wine marketer Dave Ready in 1985 to form a family owned winery located in Sonoma County's Alexander Valley. A lively and knowledgeable trio, the partners combined creative vision, hard work, and expertise to form their dynamic wine estate. Murphy-Goode quickly earned a reputation for consistently excellent, stylish wines.

Contemporary farming and incomparable grapes are paramount to Murphy-Goode's success. Estate vines grow on three Alexander Valley sites: Murphy-Goode Vineyard, Murphy Ranch, and River Ranch. Selected neighboring vineyards also provide long-term grape sources to meet the continuing demand for Murphy-Goode Estate Winery wines.

ASIAN FLAVORED NOODLES

This is a quick and simple dish when you hear the Orient calling.

DRESSING:

3^1/$_2$ tablespoons sesame oil

3^1/$_2$ tablespoons soy sauce

2 tablespoons sugar

1^1/$_2$ tablespoons Chinese black vinegar

1 tablespoon chile oil

1 teaspoon salt

12 ounces fresh Chinese egg noodles, cooked in boiling salted water until al dente, then drained

5 scallions, thinly sliced

2 tablespoons sesame seeds, lightly toasted

In a large bowl, whisk together the dressing ingredients until smooth. Add the hot noodles to the dressing and toss until well coated. Sprinkle with scallions and sesame seeds. Serve at room temperature.

Serves 4
Serve with Murphy-Goode Estate Winery Chardonnay

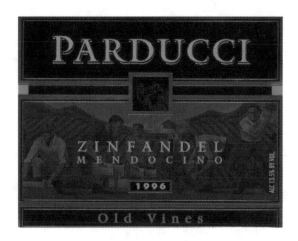

PARDUCCI WINE ESTATES

There are only two things you need to know about a wine. First, do you like it? Second, can you afford it? The people at Parducci are confident that, after tasting and pricing Parducci Wines, the answer to both questions will be an emphatic "YES."

They have always recognized that wine customers enjoy a variety of wines. As such, they have taken advantage of the numerous varieties grown in Mendocino County and produce the following wines: Cabernet Sauvignon, Chenin Blanc, Pinot Noir, Chardonnay, Charbono, Barbera, Petite Sirah, Merlot, Sauvignon Blanc, Zinfandel, Syrah, and Sangiovese. Parducci strives to bring out the varietal characteristics each grape has to offer. Wine is an honest, natural product that should never be over-processed. It should have a softness that invites pleasant consumption upon release.

SPICY CASHEW NOODLES

Cashews give a creamy richness to this dish.

3/4 cup chopped cashews

1/4 cup lightly packed cilantro leaves

3 scallions, chopped

3 tablespoons sugar

2 tablespoons rice vinegar

1 tablespoon sesame oil

1 teaspoon minced garlic

1 teaspoon minced fresh ginger

1/2 teaspoon sambal oelek or other hot chile paste

1/4 cup soy sauce

12 ounces Chinese noodles or spaghetti, cooked in boiling salted water until al dente, then drained

In the bowl of a food processor, combine cashews, cilantro, scallions, sugar, rice vinegar, sesame oil, garlic, ginger, and sambal oelek and process until smooth.

With motor running, add soy sauce and process until thoroughly combined. Pour mixture into a large serving bowl. Add the hot noodles and toss well. Serve immediately.

Serves 4 to 6
Serve with Parducci Wine Estates
Zinfandel

QUAIL RIDGE CELLARS AND VINEYARDS

Quail Ridge Cellars and Vineyards, Napa Valley's rustic gem, is nestled snugly in mid-Napa Valley. Quail Ridge's comfortable setting provides a welcome respite from the crowded surroundings of larger Napa wineries. Quail Ridge produces a number of excellent varietals, which have won numerous medals in international wine competitions.

Located off Highway 29 on a 9-acre vineyard in the town of Rutherford, Quail Ridge is an integral part of the storied Rutherford Bench growing region. From its redwood deck, it is possible to enjoy the beauty and grandeur of the majestic Mayacamas mountain range, the historical divider of Napa and Sonoma Counties.

CHILE SHRIMP
with Coconut Noodles

The rich coconut milk and the sweet and sour shrimp lends this dish a Southeast Asian flavor.

1 cup coconut milk

12 ounces wide rice stick noodles

3/4 cup sweet chile sauce

1/4 cup tomato sauce

1 tablespoon rice vinegar

2 teaspoons sugar

1 tablespoon cornstarch

1/4 cup water

2 tablespoons vegetable oil

5 shallots, finely minced

1 tablespoon minced fresh ginger

3 cloves garlic, minced

1 pound large shelled raw shrimp

(recipe continued on next page)

In a saucepan, simmer coconut milk over medium heat until reduced by half. Soak noodles in hot water for about 15 minutes, or until tender, then drain. Add the noodles to the reduced coconut milk and simmer until slightly thickened. Keep warm and set aside.

In a bowl, stir together the sweet chile sauce, tomato sauce, vinegar, and sugar. In a small bowl, whisk together the cornstarch and water until smooth. Stir into the chile sauce mixture until smooth. Set aside.

In a wok or skillet, heat oil over medium heat. Add shallots, ginger, and garlic and stir-fry until fragrant. Add the shrimp and stir-fry until shrimp turn pink. Stir in the reserved chile mixture and simmer until mixture thickens.

Divide noodles into 4 shallow bowls and spoon chile shrimp over the top. Serve immediately.

Serves 4
Serve with Quail Ridge Cellars and Vineyards
Chardonnay

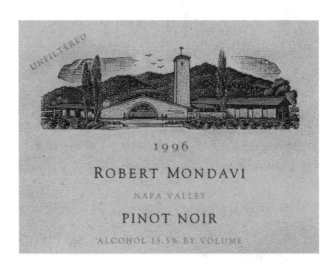

UNFILTERED

1996

ROBERT MONDAVI

NAPA VALLEY

PINOT NOIR

ALCOHOL 13.5% BY VOLUME

ROBERT MONDAVI WINERY

Founded in 1966 by Robert Mondavi and his son, Michael, the Robert Mondavi Winery is considered a leader in the modern wine industry. The Mondavis are committed to producing naturally balanced wines of great finesse and elegance that complement and enhance fine food. They have been successful in achieving these goals through Earth-friendly farming practices, a sophisticated winery emphasizing gentle treatment of their wines, and a genuine love for their handiwork. No other winery epitomizes the Napa Valley like the Robert Mondavi Winery.

GRILLED BEEF
& CELLOPHANE
NOODLE SALAD

Salads are a huge part of wine country summer entertaining. Try this one the next time you have friends over for a casual afternoon.

DRESSING:

1/4 cup fish sauce

1/4 cup freshly squeezed lime juice

2 tablespoons minced lemon grass, pale tender part only

2 tablespoons minced fresh mint

2 tablespoons palm sugar or brown sugar

4 scallions, finely chopped

2 shallots, minced

3 cloves garlic, minced

2 small hot red chiles, seeded and minced

2 teaspoons soy sauce

1/4 cup vegetable oil

8 ounces cellophane noodles

1 (1-pound) flank steak

2 tablespoons vegetable oil

Salt and freshly ground black pepper to taste

1 head of Romaine lettuce, torn into bite-sized pieces

In a large bowl, whisk together the fish sauce, lime juice, lemon grass, mint, sugar, scallions, shallots, garlic, chiles, and soy sauce. Whisk in the oil. Reserve 1/3 cup of the dressing.

Soak the noodles in hot water for 15 minutes, or until tender. Drain, then add to the dressing and toss well.

Prepare the grill. Rub the beef with the oil, then season with salt and pepper. Place on hot grill and sear on both sides until the beef is medium rare. Remove from the grill and let rest 10 minutes before carving.

Divide the lettuce onto 6 plates and place the noodles on top. Slice the flank steak thinly across the grain and fan onto the noodles. Drizzle the remaining dressing over the top.

Serves 6
Serve with Robert Mondavi Winery
Pinto Noir

RODNEY STRONG
VINEYARDS

Over 35 years ago Rodney Strong was one of the first to recognize Sonoma County's potential for excellence. After searching for vineyard land that would bring each grape variety to its fullest potential, Rodney Strong finally selected vineyard sites in the Chalk Hill, Alexander Valley, and Russian River Valley appellations to produce his wine. In the cellar, he employs the subtle use of barrel and stainless steel fermentation, oak aging, and other winemaking techniques to bring out the best in the fruit. It is his philosophy to allow the grapes from each vineyard to express their individual character in the final bottled wine.

CHICKEN YAKISOBA

Fresh yakisoba noodles can be found in the vegetable section of many supermarkets.

$^1/_2$ cup soy sauce

$^1/_3$ cup sake

1 tablespoon sugar

1 tablespoon sesame oil

4 skinless, boneless chicken breasts, cut into $^1/_2$-inch cubes

1 tablespoon cornstarch

$^1/_4$ cup vegetable oil, divided

1 onion, cut in half then thinly sliced

3 cups shredded cabbage

1 tablespoon minced garlic

1 tablespoon minced fresh ginger

1 pound fresh yakisoba noodles

3 scallions, thinly sliced

In a small bowl whisk together soy sauce, sake, sugar, and sesame oil. Set aside.

In a bowl, combine diced chicken, 2 tablespoons of the soy sauce mixture, and cornstarch. Mix well, cover and let marinate for 1 hour.

(recipe continued on next page)

In a large wok or skillet, heat 1 tablespoon of the oil over high heat. When almost smoking, add chicken and stir-fry until cooked. Remove chicken to a bowl. Add 1 tablespoon of oil to wok and add the onion and cabbage and stir-fry until very tender. Add vegetables to chicken. Add the remaining 2 tablespoons of oil to the wok and add garlic and ginger. Stir-fry until fragrant. Add noodles and stir-fry for about 3 minutes, or until they are beginning to brown. Pour in reserved soy sauce mixture and stir. Add reserved chicken and vegetables and stir-fry until heated through and liquid has been absorbed. Serve topped with sliced scallions.

Serves 6
Serve with Rodney Strong Vineyards
Pinot Noir

V. SATTUI WINERY

V. Sattui Winery is a family-owned winery estab-lished in 1885, and located in St. Helena, the very heart of California's famous Napa Valley. Their award-winning wines are sold exclusively at the winery, by mail order, and from their website direct to customers. Surrounding the beautiful stone win-ery is a large tree-shaded picnic ground. V. Sattui also boasts a large gourmet cheese shop and deli.

SESAME CRUSTED
TOFU *with Noodles*

In this light and flavorful summer dish, the crunch of the sesame seeds contrasts deliciously with the silky creaminess of the tofu.

1 (14-ounce) package extra firm tofu, drained

1/4 cup sake

2 tablespoons soy sauce

1 teaspoon sesame oil

DRESSING:

2 tablespoons prepared black bean sauce

2 tablespoons sake

2 tablespoons sesame oil

1 tablespoon soy sauce

1 tablespoon sugar

12 ounces dried Chinese egg noodles or vermicelli

2 bunches watercress, coarsely chopped

1 bunch scallions, thinly sliced

1/4 cup sesame seeds

3 tablespoons vegetable oil

Slice tofu crosswise into 8 pieces. Drain on paper towels. In a shallow dish, stir together sake, soy sauce, and sesame oil. Place tofu in dish, cover, and marinate in the refrigerator for 2 hours or overnight. Remove tofu from marinade and drain briefly. Reserve excess marinade.

For the dressing: In a large bowl, whisk together all dressing ingredients until smooth. Add reserved marinade.

Cook noodles in boiling salted water until al dente, then drain. Place hot noodles in dressing and toss to coat. Add watercress and scallions and toss to mix.

Place sesame seeds on a plate. Dip tofu into sesame seeds and press lightly to coat one side. In a large skillet, heat vegetable oil over medium heat. Cook tofu, sesame seed side down, for about 3 minutes or until golden brown. Turn and cook on the other side until golden brown.

To serve, divide noodles between 4 plates and place 2 pieces of tofu, sesame seed side up, on top of each.

Serves 4
Serve with V. Sattui Winery
Sauvignon Blanc

SEAVEY VINEYARD

More than 120 years ago the vineyards the Seaveys now cultivate were planted with grapes to make "claret of high repute," judged by the St. Helena Star of that day to be "as fine as one might find anywhere." This was back when Conn Valley Road was little more than a wagon trail and the label of the wine was "Franco-Swiss Cellar" under the ownership of G. Crochat & Co. After the breakup of the company in the early 1900s, no more grapes were grown on the property until Bill and Mary Seavey acquired it and began to replant the vineyards in 1981, with Chardonnay in the cooler areas along Conn Creek, and Cabernet Sauvignon on the adjoining south-facing hillsides. In 1986, the Seaveys acquired land above their property and added small blocs of Merlot, Cabernet Franc, and Petite Verdot as well as more Cabernet Sauvignon for a current total of 38 acres of vineyard. In 1990 they completed renovation of the 1881 stone barn as their small winery, and began selecting grapes for limited lots of estate produced Cabernet Sauvignon and Chardonnay.

STEAMED ALBACORE TUNA DUMPLINGS
with Spicy Ginger-Lime Beurre Blanc

When you have a beautiful piece of fresh tuna like the one given to us by our good friend and neighbor, Arthur Seavey, you only want to enhance the delicate flavor with subtle seasonings.

STEAMED ALBACORE TUNA DUMPLINGS:

1 scallion, minced

1 tablespoon soy sauce

2 teaspoons mirin

1 teaspoon minced garlic

1 teaspoon minced fresh ginger

1 teaspoon sugar

1 pound fresh albacore tuna, finely diced

1 egg, lightly beaten

1 tablespoon water

Round wonton wrappers

(recipe continued on next page)

SPICY GINGER-LIME BEURRE BLANC:

1 teaspoon vegetable oil

1 tablespoon minced shallots

1 teaspoon minced fresh ginger

1/4 cup Seavey Vineyard Chardonnay

Juice of 1 lime

1/3 cup heavy cream

1/4 cup cold butter, cut into small pieces

1/4 cup sweet chile sauce

Salt to taste

For the dumplings: In a bowl, whisk together the scallion, soy sauce, mirin, garlic, ginger, and sugar until the sugar dissolves. Add the tuna and gently toss together until evenly mixed.

In a small bowl, whisk together lightly beaten egg and 1 tablespoon water to make an egg wash. Place a wonton wrapper on a lightly floured surface and brush lightly with egg wash. Place a tablespoon of filling in the center of the wrapper. Bring the edges up around the filling to completely enclose the filling. Gently twist the top to seal the dumpling. Slightly flatten the bottom so that the dumpling will stand upright. Place the dumpling on a lightly floured baking sheet. Repeat until all of the filling is used.

For the beurre blanc: In a small saucepan, heat the oil over medium heat. Add the shallots, and ginger and sauté until tender. Stir in the wine and lime juice and simmer until almost all of the liquid has evaporated. Whisk in the cream and simmer until reduced by half. Reduce heat to low, and whisk in the butter, one piece at a time until all is incorporated. Stir in the chile sauce and season with salt. Keep barely warm; if the sauce gets too hot, it will separate.

To steam the dumplings: Transfer dumplings to several lightly oiled heatproof plates that will fit inside the racks of a bamboo steamer. Place the dumplings in the steaming racks. Bring a pot of water to a boil and place the bamboo steamer racks on top of the pot. Cover and steam for 15 to 20 minutes. Serve immediately with the beurre blanc.

Makes 48 dumplings
Serve with Seavey Vineyard
Chardonnay

STERLING
VINEYARDS

Built in the architectural style of the Greek Island of Mykonos, the Sterling Vineyards winery sits dramatically on top of a 300-foot knoll just south of Napa Valley's northernmost town, Calistoga. Its white, monastic buildings contrast sharply with the dark green of the trees that cover the knoll. Visitors are carried up to the winery by aerial tramway and treated to a spectacular view of the Napa Valley below, as well as a close-up look at the Napa Valley's most dramatic and recognizable winery. The panorama is awe-inspiring and peaceful, punctuated only by the peal of Sterling's antique English church bells.

ROASTED CHINESE DUCK POTSTICKERS
with Peach Dipping Sauce

If you have the good fortune to live close to an ethnic center, look for the rich mahogany-colored ducks hanging in the window of the Chinese grocery stores.

PEACH DIPPING SAUCE:

2 peaches, peeled and chopped

1/4 cup chicken stock

2 tablespoons rice vinegar

1 tablespoon brown sugar

1 tablespoon soy sauce

1 teaspoon minced garlic

1 teaspoon minced fresh ginger

ROASTED CHINESE DUCK POTSTICKERS:

1 Chinese roasted duck

1/3 cup finely minced water chestnuts

2 scallions, minced

2 tablespoons hoisin sauce

1 tablespoon sake

1 teaspoon honey

1 teaspoon soy sauce

(recipe continued on next page)

1 egg, lightly beaten

1 tablespoon water

Round wonton wrappers

3 tablespoons vegetable oil

Water

For the dipping sauce: Place chopped peaches in the bowl of a food processor and process until smooth. Transfer to a saucepan. Add chicken stock, vinegar, brown sugar, soy sauce, garlic, and ginger to the saucepan. Simmer over medium heat until slightly thickened. Remove from heat and cool completely. Set aside.

For the potstickers: Remove the skin and meat of the legs and breast of the duck. Save the remainder for another use. There will be a thick layer of fat clinging under the skin. Place the skin, fat-side up, on a cutting board. With the back of a knife, scrape off the fat and discard it. Finely chop the skin and meat and transfer to a bowl. Add the water chestnuts, scallions, hoisin sauce, sake, honey, and soy sauce and mix well.

In a small bowl, whisk together lightly beaten egg and 1 tablespoon water to make an egg wash. Place a wonton wrapper on a lightly floured surface and brush lightly with egg wash. Place a tablespoon of filling in the center of the wrapper and fold over to make a half moon shape. Pinch the top together at midpoint. Working from the edge, pleat the dough toward the center, making 3 pleats on each side so the potsticker will be completely sealed. Slightly flatten the bottom so that the potsticker will stand upright. Place the potsticker, pleated edge up, on a lightly floured baking sheet. Repeat until all of the filling is used.

In a large nonstick skillet, heat the oil over medium-high heat. Arrange the potstickers in the skillet in a closely packed circle, pleated sides up. Cook until the edges begin to brown. Add enough water to come halfway up the sides of the pot-stickers. Take care since the oil will splatter a bit. Cover the skillet and reduce the heat to medium. Cook for 6 to 8 minutes to steam the potstickers. Remove the lid and continue to cook until all the liquid has evaporated and the potstickers begin to sizzle in the remaining oil. When the bottoms are well browned and crisp, transfer to a serving plate. Divide the dipping sauce into small individual bowls. Serve immediately.

Makes about 36
Serve with Sterling Vineyards
Merlot

TREFETHEN VINEYARDS

Tradition combines with technology at Trefethen Vineyards, where a century-old winery and the latest in winemaking equipment give the Trefethen family, and their wines, the best of both worlds.

First planted to grapes in the 1850s, the Eshcol ranch, as it was known back then, received its name from a biblical allusion to an immense cluster of grapes. In 1968 Gene and Katie Trefethen revitalized the old Eshcol property and planted new vines on the 600-acre valley estate and on 50 acres to the northwest. The first wines were vinified in 1973, and today wine production has climbed to 75,000 cases per year.

The Trefethen family has this to say about their wines: "Winemaking is part agriculture and part parenting. We are proud to introduce you to what we have worried over and cared for—our wines. They are meant to be shared and enjoyed among friends."

RED SNAPPER
with Sweet and Spicy Tamarind Sauce

The turmeric gives the snapper a pleasing yellow hue, while the tamarind sauce provides a blast of flavor.

2 tablespoons cornstarch

1 teaspoon turmeric

1/2 teaspoon salt

1/4 teaspoon white pepper

1/3 cup vegetable oil, divided

1 pound, 4 ounces red snapper, cut into 1-inch cubes

SWEET AND SPICY TAMARIND SAUCE:

1/2 cup hot water

2 tablespoons dried tamarind

2 tablespoons vegetable oil

1 cup chopped onion

3 cloves garlic, minced

1 stalk lemon grass, pale tender part only, minced

1 small hot red chile, seeded and minced

1/2 teaspoon shrimp paste

1 cup chicken stock

1 tablespoon sugar

1 teaspoon salt

(recipe continued on next page)

1 tablespoon cornstarch

3 tablespoons water

1 pound wide rice noodles, soaked in hot water until tender, then drained

2 scallions, thinly sliced diagonally

🍂 In a bowl, stir together cornstarch, turmeric, salt, and pepper with a fork until blended. Stir in 2 tablespoons of the oil until smooth. Add the cubed fish and toss until evenly coated. Set aside.

For the sauce: In a small bowl, combine hot water and tamarind. Let stand 30 minutes, then strain and discard solids. Set aside the tamarind liquid.

In a skillet, heat 2 tablespoons of the oil over medium-high heat. Add the onion, garlic, lemon grass, chile, and shrimp paste and stir-fry until fragrant. Reduce heat to medium and stir in reserved tamarind liquid, chicken stock, sugar, and salt. Simmer until the liquid is reduced by half. In a small bowl, stir together cornstarch and 3 tablespoons water until smooth. Stir cornstarch mixture into the sauce and simmer until the sauce has slightly thickened. Reduce heat to low and keep the sauce warm.

In a large wok or skillet, heat the remaining 1/2 cup oil over high heat. When the oil is hot, add the fish and stir-fry until cooked through and crisp on the outside.

Toss the noodles with the sauce and divide onto 6 plates. Top with red snapper and sprinkle with scallions. Serve immediately.

Serves 6
Serve with Trefethen Vineyards
Napa Valley Chardonnay

Wine comes in at the mouth
And love comes in at the eye;
That's all we shall know for truth
Before we grow old and die.
Yeats

SUTTER HOME
WINERY

Sutter Home is one of California's enviable success stories. Begun in 1874, the winery passed into the hands of its current family owners in 1947 when John and Mario Trinchero immigrated from Italy and set down roots in the Napa Valley. Today their children carry on this once mom-and-pop operation.

A milestone occurred in 1972 when, in an effort to make his red Zinfandel more robust, Bob Trinchero drew off some of the free run juice and fermented it as a "white" wine. This pale pink Zinfandel became a favorite at the winery's tasting room, and thus was born White Zinfandel. Today Sutter Home is known not only for their popular White Zinfandel, but also for their high-quality, affordable varietal wines as well as their line of nonalcoholic wines.

RICE NOODLES
with Vegetables
& Spicy Peanut Sauce

Jeffrey Starr, executive chef of Sutter Home Winery, researched which Asian flavors would perfectly complement their Gewürztraminer and came up with this outstanding recipe.

SPICY PEANUT SAUCE:

1/4 cup sesame oil

3 tablespoons hoisin sauce

2 tablespoons peanut butter

2 tablespoons rice vinegar

1 tablespoon chile oil

1 tablespoon minced fresh cilantro

1 tablespoon freshly squeezed lime juice

1 tablespoon minced scallions

1 tablespoon sesame seeds

1 tablespoon soy sauce

1 tablespoon sugar

1 tablespoon brown sugar

1 1/2 teaspoons Dijon mustard

1 1/2 teaspoons tomato paste

3/4 teaspoon dried red chile flakes

(recipe continued on next page)

3/4 teaspoon Chinese five spice powder

1/2 teaspoon salt

1 pound rice noodles, cooked according to package directions, then drained

1/4 cup vegetable oil, divided

1 cup broccoli florets

1 carrot, thinly sliced

8 mushrooms, sliced

1 red bell pepper, julienned

1 zucchini, thinly sliced

3 scallions, thinly sliced

For the sauce: In the bowl of a food processor, combine all sauce ingredients and process until smooth. Set aside.

Toss hot noodles with 2 tablespoons of the vegetable oil until lightly coated and set aside.

In a skillet, heat remaining 2 tablespoons of the vegetable oil over high heat. Add the broccoli, carrot, mushrooms, bell pepper, and zucchini and stir-fry until crisp-tender. Reduce heat to medium and stir in reserved sauce until coated. Add the noodles and toss to coat. Divide into 4 shallow bowls and sprinkle with scallions. Serve immediately.

Serves 4
Serve with Sutter Home Winery
Gewürztraminer

Worries enough come all the time,
And the cure therefore is the
beloved vine.

Johann Wolfgang von Goethe

THE WINERIES:

Beaulieu Vineyard
1960 St. Helena Highway
Rutherford, CA 94573
707.963.2411

Belvedere Vineyards and Winery
435 West Dry Creek Road
Healdsburg, CA 95448
707.433.8236

Benziger Family Winery
1883 London Ranch Road
Glen Ellen, CA 95442
707.935.3000

Beringer Vineyards
2000 Main Street
St. Helena, CA 94574
707.963.7115

Cardinale Winery
Post Office Box 328
Oakville, CA 94562
707.944.2807

Cedar Mountain Winery
7000 Tesla Road
Livermore, CA 94550
510.373.6694

Chateau Montelena Winery
1429 Tubbs Lane
Calistoga, CA 94515
707.942.5105

Clos Pegase Winery
1060 Dunaweal Lane
Calistoga, CA 94515
707.942.4981

De Loach Vineyards
1791 Olivet Road
Santa Rosa, CA 95401
707.526.9111

Domaine Carneros
1240 Duhig Road
Napa, CA 94559
707.257.3020

Dry Creek Vineyard
3770 Lambert Bridge Road
Healdsburg, CA 95448
707.433.1000

Duckhorn Vineyards
1000 Lodi Lane
St. Helena, CA 94574
707.963.7108

Ferrari-Carano Winery
8761 Dry Creek Road
Healdsburg, CA 95448
707.433.6700

Geyser Peak Winery
22281 Chianti Road
Geyserville, CA 95441
707.857.9463

Glen Ellen Winery
14301 Arnold Drive
Glen Ellen, CA 95442
707.939.6277

Gloria Ferrer Champagne Caves
23555 Highway 121
Sonoma, CA 95476
707.996.7256

Grgich Hills Cellar
1829 St. Helena Highway
Rutherford, CA 94573
707.963.2784

Kendall-Jackson Winery
5007 Fulton Road
Santa Rosa, CA 95439
707.571.8100

Kenwood Vineyards
9592 Sonoma Highway
Kenwood, CA 95452
707.833.5891

Korbel Champagne Cellars
13250 River Road
Guerneville, CA 95446
707.824.7000

Ledson Vineyards and Winery
7335 Sonoma Highway
Kenwood, CA 95452
707.833.2330

Mark West Estate Vineyards
   and Winery
7010 Trenton-Healdsburg Road
Forestville, CA 95436
707.544.4813

Martini and Prati Winery
2191 Laguna Road
Santa Rosa, CA 95401
707.823.2404

Mumm Cuvée Napa
8445 Silverado Trail
Rutherford, CA 94573
707.942.3434

Murphy-Goode Estate Winery
4001 Highway 128
Geyserville, CA 95441
707.431.7644

Navarro Vineyards
5601 Highway 128
Philo, CA 95466
707.895.3686

Parducci Wine Estates
501 Parducci Road
Ukiah, CA 95482
707.463.5350

Quail Ridge Cellars and
Vineyards
1155 Mee Lane
Rutherford, CA 94573
707.963.9783

Robert Mondavi Winery
7801 St. Helena Highway
Oakville, CA 94562
707.226.1395

Rodney Strong Vineyards
11455 Old Redwood Highway
Healdsburg, CA 95448
707.433.6521

Seavey Vineyard
1310 Conn Valley Road
St. Helena, CA 94574
707.963.8339

Sterling Vineyards
1111 Dunaweal Lane
Calistoga, CA 94515
707.942.3300

Sutter Home Winery
100 St. Helena Highway, South
St. Helena, CA 94574
707.963.3104

Trefethen Vineyards
1160 Oak Knoll Avenue
Napa, CA 94558
707.255.7700

Turnbull Wine Cellars
8210 St. Helena Highway
Oakville, CA 94562
800.887.6285

V. Sattui Winery
1111 White Lane
St. Helena, CA 94574
707.963.7774

THE CATERERS:

Night Owl Catering
Post Office Box 226
Sebastapol, CA 95472
707.823.1850

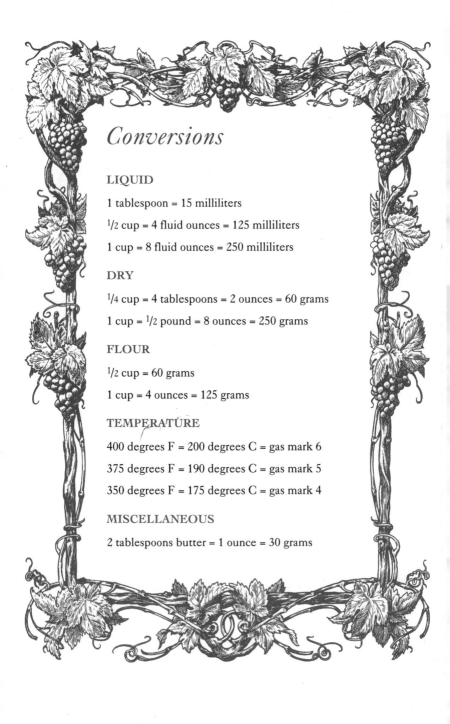

Conversions

LIQUID

1 tablespoon = 15 milliliters

$^1/_2$ cup = 4 fluid ounces = 125 milliliters

1 cup = 8 fluid ounces = 250 milliliters

DRY

$^1/_4$ cup = 4 tablespoons = 2 ounces = 60 grams

1 cup = $^1/_2$ pound = 8 ounces = 250 grams

FLOUR

$^1/_2$ cup = 60 grams

1 cup = 4 ounces = 125 grams

TEMPERATURE

400 degrees F = 200 degrees C = gas mark 6

375 degrees F = 190 degrees C = gas mark 5

350 degrees F = 175 degrees C = gas mark 4

MISCELLANEOUS

2 tablespoons butter = 1 ounce = 30 grams